DRUM EDITION
METALLICA

RIDE THE LIGHTNING

As recorded by METALLICA
on ELEKTRA Records

Management: Q Prime, Inc.
Transcribed by Howard Fields
Edited by Jon Chappell
Music Engraving by W.R. Music
Production Manager: Daniel Rosenbaum
Art Direction: Kerstin Fairbend
Director of Music: Mark Phillips

Photography by Ross Halfin

C O N T E N T S

ISBN: 0-89524-610-4

Copyright © 1992 Cherry Lane Music Company, Inc.
International Copyright Secured All Rights Reserved

cherry lane
music company

EXCLUSIVELY DISTRIBUTED BY
HAL•LEONARD®
CORPORATION
7777 W. BLUEMOUND RD. P.O. BOX 13819 MILWAUKEE, WI 53213

LARS ULRICH:
RIDE THE LIGHTNING

As drummer, songwriter and founder of Metallica, Lars Ulrich has elevated this unique band to the top of the speed metal thrash pile. By now, the band's catalogue ... *And Justice for All*, *Master of Puppets*, *Ride the Lightning* and *Kill 'Em All*—has defined and redefined American heavy metal. Along with innovative musical ideas on each album is an impressive array of Ulrich's flawlessly executed drumming techniques.

Unlike the many musicians whose careers are carved practically at birth, Lars, following in his father's footsteps, was a Top 10 ranked tennis player as a teenager in his native Denmark. But in 1973, after his dad took him to a Deep Purple concert, Lars bought the group's *Fireball* album—and a transformation began. In 1980, Lars moved to Los Angeles with his father to promote his tennis career, but it didn't take long for them to realize that Lars' respectable European ranking meant little in the ferociously competitive U.S. tennis circuit. It was then that the music took over.

In 1981, Lars called up an acquaintance, James Hetfield, who shared his restlessness, pent-up energy and fervor for the likes of Iron Maiden, Def Leppard and Motorhead. With that phone call, Metallica was born. The band played their first gigs in the spring of 1982, got a record deal not long after that and, in 1983, recorded their debut album, *Kill 'Em All*—even though Lars had been playing drums seriously for only three years.

As Lars candidly admits, the band's first recorded effort was lacking in technical and creative prowess. Indeed, the second album, *Ride the Lightning*, was a profound change for the better. It would probably be hard to find two consecutive albums in any band's catalogue that show a metamorphosis as dramatic as Metallica's progression from *Kill 'Em All* to *Ride the Lightning*.

"The year we wrote most of the songs for *Ride the Lightning*, we were ready to broaden our horizons quite a bit musically," says Lars. "I remember clearly how one day a few of us were saying to each other, 'Well, we really can't play,' and it was like 'Well, let's try and learn how.' So Kirk took lessons from this guy that nobody knew at the time, [guitar virtuoso] Joe Satriani, and I took lessons from his drummer. When I met him I said, 'Hello. I've toured all over the world, I have an album out, but I can't play drums.' Basically everybody went back to the drawing board and *Ride the Lightning* emerged."

It may inspire many players to realize that even a musician of Lars Ulrich's caliber went through this period of low self-confidence. "After *Kill 'Em All* I became pretty uncomfortable with my playing ability," says Lars. "I really worked a lot on developing my drumming style to make it looser and more progressive. I'd wake up and just play my drum kit all day."

The licks Lars developed during this period of insecurity led to the respect and admiration he enjoys today as one of the finest heavy metal drummers around. As he admits, "The biggest foot forward in my drumming happened between *Kill 'Em All* and *Ride the Lightning*."

Most prominent and impressive in the arsenal of techniques Lars learned during this time are the thunderous, machine gun–like double bass drum sixteenth-note rhythm patterns that have since come to be expected of any drummer who dares to sit behind two bass drums. The power and precision with which he plays the pattern can be heard on the songs "Ride the Lightning," "The Call of Ktulu," "Fade to Black" (on which Lars keeps the bass drums moving this way for the last 39 bars of the song, right into the fade out) nd "Trapped Under Ice," on which he rides bass drum sixteenths throughout nearly the entire tune. The first recorded song in which Lars employed this technique is "Fight Fire with Fire." Most clearly heard on the solo drums section following the guitar solo, it is excerpted here:

"Fight Fire with Fire " 12 bars before 4th verse

Says Lars of this passage, "This was my proudest moment on the sixteenth notes because, at the time, there was nobody who had played sixteenths that fast on any record. The song 'Overkill' on the Motorhead album of the same name, which featured drummer Phil Taylor, was the first song that had sixteenth notes cruising all the way through. Obviously people like Bill Ward [Black Sabbath] and, going back further, Ian Paice [Deep Purple] used double bass, but Phil Taylor was one of the first people I was inspired by. 'Fight Fire with Fire' was my answer to 'Overkill' except I played it three times as fast as anybody I'd ever heard, and I remember a lot of people were really blown away with that 'cause we're talking 1984 here."

It should be emphasized that Lars did not simply wake up one morning and find himself able to execute this pattern: It took intense practice and great discipline. One of his biggest challenges was in developing the proper coordination: Says Lars, "Some guys can sit down and their left hand can go in a completely different frame than their right foot without even thinking, or they can have four different things going on at once, all very naturally. But I always felt almost spastic in that I couldn't coordinate the left hand and right foot. When I tried to make them hit at the same time, I'd fall off the stool ... the whole coordination thing took me a really long time. I had to start everything slowly. Without sounding like a drum teacher, that's the way to do everything: strip it down to its absolute bare essentials and get it tight at a really slow, tedious tempo. Then it's just a matter of working it up into whatever tempo you want to take it to."

Another engaging and effective technique Lars employed on *Ride the Lightning* is a fill—sixteenth notes on the hands played against sixteenths on the bass drums. The fill always comes between bars of a hi-hat/snare ride pattern with the same double bass sixteenths. Here are two examples of this from "Trapped Under Ice":

"Trapped Under Ice" 2 bars before Guitar solo I

Guitar solo I

"Trapped Under Ice" 3 bars before the D.S.

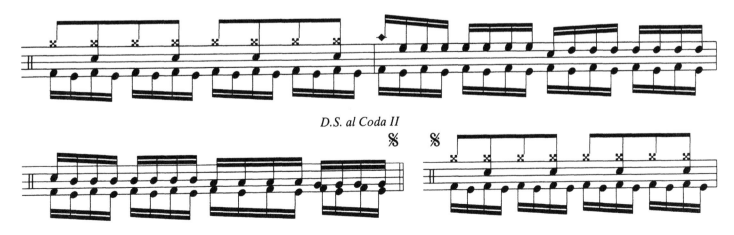

D.S. al Coda II

Apart from Lars' double bass expertise he also perpetuates the phenomenal single bass drum techniques he began on *Kill 'Em All*, particularly the use of triplets. Here are two examples of the use of single bass drum triplets on *Ride the Lightning*:

"Fight Fire with Fire" 1st and 2nd Verses: bar 1

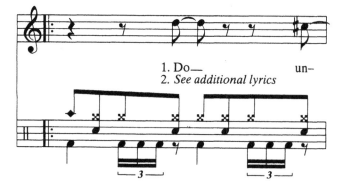

1. Do— un—
2. *See additional lyrics*

"Fade to Black" 1 bar before 1st bridge

Ride the Lightning is full of examples which prove that 1983 was without a doubt a pivotal period in Lars Ulrich's development as a drummer. His formidable technical and creative powers came to the fore that year, and have continued to do so ever since.

—Howard Fields

Howard Fields was the drummer for the late Harry Chapin from 1975-81.
He continues to be actively involved in touring, recording and teaching.

The Drum Set-up of Lars Ulrich

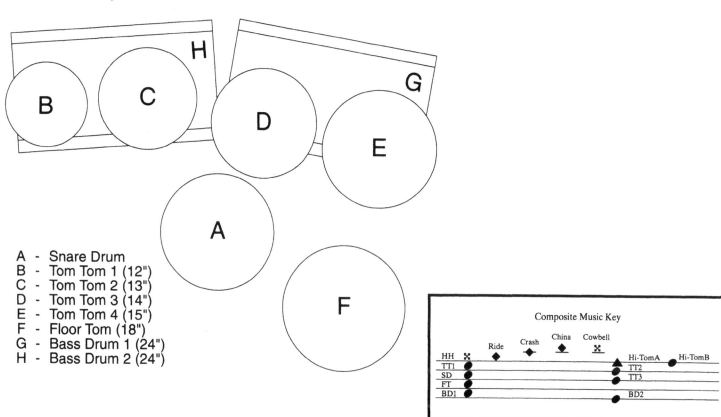

A - Snare Drum
B - Tom Tom 1 (12")
C - Tom Tom 2 (13")
D - Tom Tom 3 (14")
E - Tom Tom 4 (15")
F - Floor Tom (18")
G - Bass Drum 1 (24")
H - Bass Drum 2 (24")

DRUM NOTATION EXPLANATION

HI-HAT

OPEN AND CLOSED HI-HAT:
Strike the open hi-hat on notes labeled with an *o*. Strike the closed hi-hat on unlabeled notes.

HI-HAT WITH FOOT:
Clap hi-hat cymbals together with foot pedal.

HI-HAT WITH SLUR:
The open hi-hat is struck and then closed with the foot on the beat indicated by the hi-hat w/foot notation below, creating a *shoop* sound.

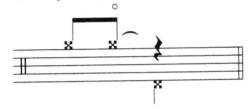

HI-HAT BARK:
The open hi-hat is struck and is immediately, almost simultaneously closed so that the *shoop* sound is severely clipped.

CYMBALS

CHOKE:
Hit the crash cymbal and catch it immediately with the other hand, producing a short, choked crash sound.

BELL OF CYMBAL:
Hit the cymbal near the center, directly on the cup or bell portion.

CYMBAL ROLL:
Play a roll on the cymbal rapidly enough to produce a sustained, uninterrupted *shhh* sound lasting for the number of beats indicated.

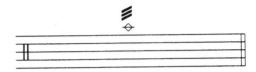

DRUMS

CROSS STICK:
Anchor the tip end of the stick on the snare drum skin at the eight o'clock position, two to three inches from the rim. Then raise and lower the butt end, striking the rim at the two o'clock position, producing a clicky woodblock-type sound.

FLAM:
Hit the drum with both sticks, one slightly after the other, producing a single, thick-sounding note.

RUFF:
Play the grace notes rapidly and as close to the principal note as possible. The grace notes are unaccented and should be played slightly before the beat. The principal note is accented and played directly on the beat.

CLOSED ROLL:
Play a roll on the snare drum creating a sustained, uninterrupted *tshhh* sound lasting for the duration of the rhythm indicated and with no break between the two tied notes.

FIGHT FIRE WITH FIRE

Words and Music by
James Hetfield, Lars Ulrich, and
Cliff Burton

*2nd and 3rd times play on bass drum on beat 1.

1st, 2nd Verses

1. Do un-to oth-ers as they've
2. *See additional lyrics*

done to you. But what the hell is

this world com-ing to?

*2nd time play on crash on beat 2.

Chorus

Fight fi-re with fi-re. End-ing is near.

Fight fi-re with fi-re. Burst-ing with fear. *(Spoken:) We all shall die!*

3rd Verse

Time is like a fuse, short and burn-ing fast.

Ar - ma - ged-don's here, like said in the past.

Chorus

Fight fi - re with fi - re. End - ing is near.

Fight fi - re with fi - re. Burst - ing with fear.

Half time feel

(end half time feel)

Guitar solo

*2nd time play ✦ ✕ on crash and hi-hat on beat 1.

9

4th Verse

Soon to fill our lungs, the hot winds of death.

The gods are laugh-ing, so take your last breath.

Chorus

Fight fi-re with fi-re. End-ing is near.

Fight fi-re with fi-re. Burst-ing with fear.

Fight fi - re with fi - re. Fight fi - re with fi - re. Fight fi - re with fi - re. Fight fi - re with fi - re.

Fight fi - re with fi - re. Fight fi - re with fi - re. Fight fi - re with fi - re.

Fight fi - re with fi - re. Fight!

Additional Lyrics

2. Blow the universe into nothingness.
   Nuclear warfare shall lay us to rest. *(To Chorus)*

RIDE THE LIGHTNING

Words and Music by
James Hetfield, Lars Ulrich,
Cliff Burton and Dave Mustaine

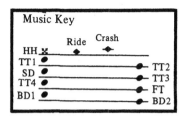

1. Guilt-y as charged. But damn it, it ain't right. There's some-one else_ con-trol-ling_ me.
2.3. *See additional lyrics*

*2nd time play ▼ on crash on beat 2.

Death in the air. Strapped in the e-lec-tric chair. This can't be hap-pen-ing to me.

*2nd & 3rd times play × on hi-hat on beats 2 and 4.

*2nd & 3rd times play on crash on beat 2.

Who made you God to say "I'll take your life from you!"

Chorus

3rd time substitute Drum Pat. 3

Flash be-fore my eyes. Now it's time to die.

3rd time to Coda

Burn - ing in my brain. I can feel the

1.

flame.

Drum Pat. 3

flame.

Double time feel

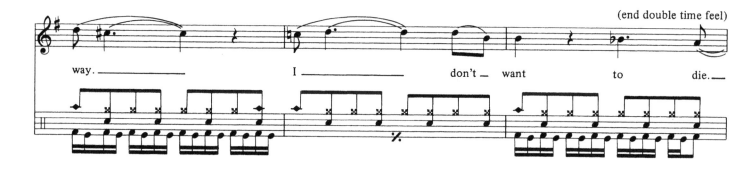

Some - one help_ me. _ Oh, please God_ help me! They're try - ing to take it all_ a-

(end double time feel)

way. _____ I _____ don't_ want to die.

Half time feel

Guitar solo

(end half time feel)

Half time feel   (end half time feel)

D.S. al Coda

Coda

flame.

Additional Lyrics

2. Wait for the sign
   To flick the switch of death.
   It's the beginning of the end.
   Sweat, chilling cold,
   As I watch death unfold.
   Consciousness my only friend.
   My fingers grip with fear.
   What am I doing here? *(To Chorus)*

3. Time moving slow.
   The minutes seem like hours.
   The final curtain call I see.
   How true is this?
   Just get it over with.
   If this is true, just let it be.
   Wakened by horrid scream.
   Freed from this frightening dream. *(To Chorus)*

FOR WHOM THE BELL TOLLS

Words and Music by
James Hetfield, Lars Ulrich
and Cliff Burton

*2nd, 3rd & 4th times play on hi-hat on beat 1.

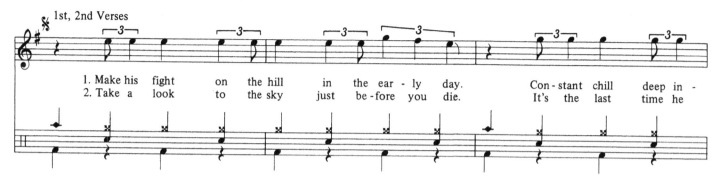

1st, 2nd Verses

1. Make his fight on the hill in the ear - ly day. Con - stant chill deep in -
2. Take a look to the sky just be - fore you die. It's the last time he

2nd time substitute Drum Pat. 1

side.
will.

Shout - ing gun, on they run through the end - less grey.
Black - ened roar, mas - sive roar fills the crum - bling sky.

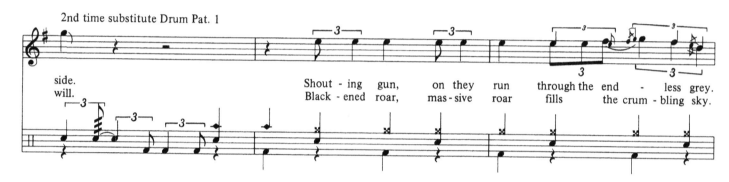

2nd time substitute Drum Pat. 2

On they fight, for they're right.___ Yes, but who's to say? For a hill men would
Shat - tered goal fills his soul ___ with a ruth - less cry. Stran - ger now are his

2nd time substitute Drum Pat. 3

kill. Why? They do not know. Suf - fered wounds test their pride.
eyes to this mys - ter - y. Hears the si - lence so loud.

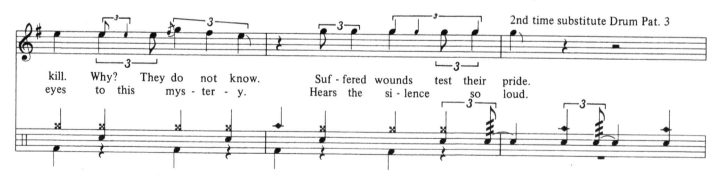

Drum Pat. 1

Drum Pat. 2

Drum Pat. 3

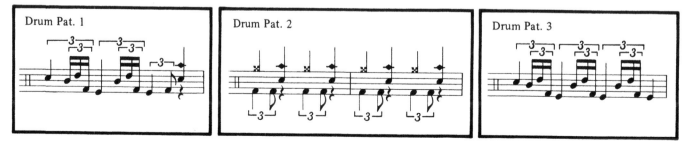

Men of five, still a - live ___ through the rag - ing glow. Gone in - sane from the pain ___
Crack of dawn, all is gone ex - cept the will to be. Now they see what will be, ___

Chorus

___ that they sure - ly know. ___ } For whom the bell ___
___ blind - ed eyes to see. ___ }

___ tolls. ___ Time march - es on

To Coda

for whom the bell ___ tolls. ___

Interlude

D.S. al Coda   Coda **Not in strict time**

Repeat and fade

FADE TO BLACK

Words and Music by
James Hetfield, Lars Ulrich
Cliff Burton and Kirk Hammett

'ry day.
_ of me.

Get - ting lost with - in___ my - self,___
Death - ly lost, this can't___ be real, ___

noth - ing mat - ters, no___ one___ else.
can - not stand this hell___ I___ feel.

I have lost the will___
Emp - ti - ness is fill -

*2nd time play on bass drum
on beat 2.

2nd time substitute Drum Pat. 2

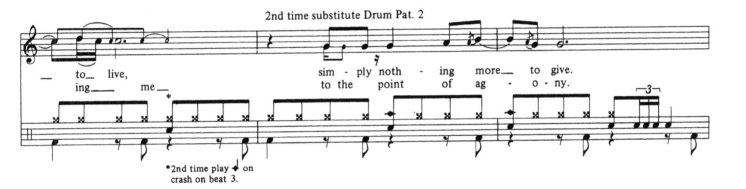

_ to___ live,
ing___ me ___

sim - ply noth - ing more___ to give.
to the point of ag - o - ny.

*2nd time play on
crash on beat 3.

There is noth - ing more___ for me.___
Grow - ing dark - ness tak - ing dawn,___

Need the end to set ___
I was me but now___

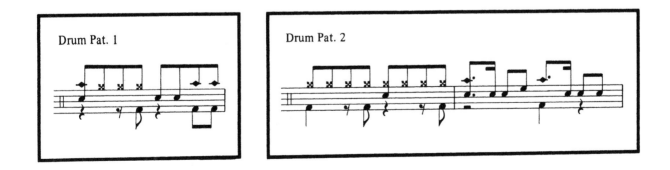

Drum Pat. 1

Drum Pat. 2

me_free.

he's   gone. _____

2nd time substitute Drum Pat. 3

2nd time substitute Drum Pat. 4

To Coda ⊕

*2nd time
play ♪♪ on TT3
on beat 4.

Interlude

D.S. al Coda 𝄋

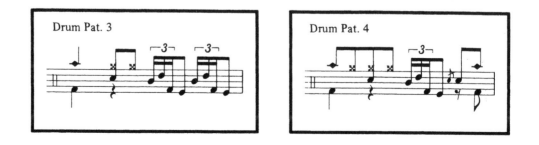

Drum Pat. 3

Drum Pat. 4

Coda **Faster** ♩ = 144

1st Bridge

No one but me can save my-self but it's too late.____

Now I can't think, think why I should e - ven____ try.____

2nd Bridge

Yes - ter - day seems as though it nev - er ex - ist - ed.____

Death greets me warm, now I will just say good-

bye.

Begin fade

Fade out

ESCAPE

Words and Music by
James Hetfield, Lars Ulrich
and Kirk Hammett

To es-cape from the true - false world. ___ Un-dam-aged des - tin - y. _____
Feed my brain with your so - called stan - dard. Who says that I ain't right? ___

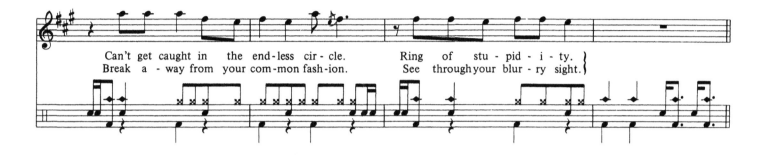

Can't get caught in the end-less cir - cle. Ring of stu - pid - i - ty.
Break a - way from your com-mon fash-ion. See through your blur - ry sight.

Chorus

Out ___ for my own; out ___ to be free. _____

One ___ with my mind, they ___ just can't see. _____

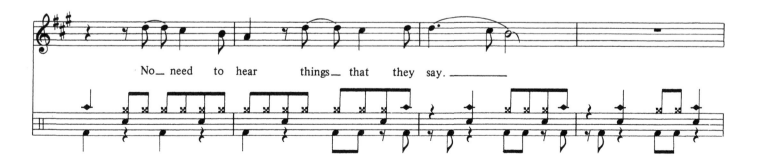

No ___ need to hear things ___ that they say. _____

29

Life's— for my own to live— my own way.———

See them try to bring the ham - mer down.

Half time feel
Bridge

(end half time feel)

No damn chains can hold me to the ground.

Guitar solo

Life's for my own to live my own way.

Life's for my own to live my own way.

Repeat and fade

Life's for my own to live my own way.

31

TRAPPED UNDER ICE

Words and Music by
James Hetfield, Lars Ulrich
and Kirk Hammett

Guitar solo II

D.S. al Coda I

Coda I ____ (end double time feel)

1.

2.

1.   2.

Bridge

(Scream) from my soul.__ (Fate.) Mys - ti - fied.__ (Hell) for - ev - er more.__

(Scream)from my soul.__ (Fate.) Mys - ti - fied.__ (Hell) for - ev - er more.__

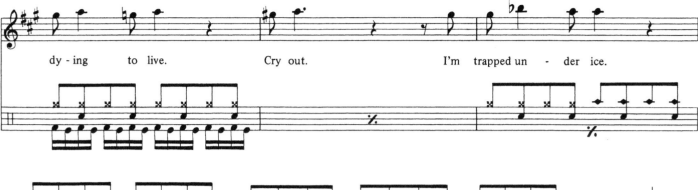

dy - ing   to live.   Cry out.   I'm trapped un - der ice.

Additional Lyrics

2. Crystalized as I lay here and rest.
   Eyes of glass stare directly at death.
   From deep sleep I have broken away.
   No one knows, no one hears what I say. *(To Chorus)*

3. No release from my cryonic state.
   What is this? I've been stricken by fate.
   Wrapped up tight, cannot move, can't break free.
   Hand of doom has a tight grip on me. *(To Chorus)*

CREEPING DEATH

Words and Music by
James Hetfield, Lars Ulrich,
Cliff Burton and Kirk Hammett

§ 1st, 2nd, 3rd Verses   3rd time substitute Drum Pat. 2

1. Slaves,   He - brews born __ to serve __   to the phar - aoh. __
2.3. *See additional lyrics*

*2nd time bass drum   *2nd time play ✗
rests on beat 4.   on hi-hat on beat 4.

2nd time substitute Drum Pat. 1
3rd time substitute Drum Pat. 3

Heed   to his ev - 'ry word, __   live in fear. __

*2nd time play ♩ on crash
on beat 4.

3rd time substitute Drum Pat. 4

Faith   of the un - known one, __   the de - liv - 'rer. __

*2nd time play ✗ on
hi-hat on beat 4.

Wait,   some - thing must __ be done, __   four hun - dred years. __

Drum Pat. 2

Drum Pat. 1

Drum Pat. 3

Drum Pat. 4

3rd time to Coda ⊕

Chorus

So let it be writ - ten.   So let it be done. ____

*2nd time play on bass drum
on beats 1 and 2.

I'm sent here by ___ the cho - sen one. ___

*2nd time play on bass drum
on beat 4.

So let it be writ - ten.   So let it be done. ____

To kill the first ___ born phar-aoh   son. ___   I'm creep - ing death. ___

1.

Guitar solo

Half time feel
Bridge

Die   by   my   hand.   I   creep   a - cross   the   land.

*2nd time play ◆ on crash on beat 3.

1.
Kill - ing   first   born   man.

2.
Kill - ing   first   born   man.

┌─3─┐   *D.S. al Coda*

Coda

Chorus

So let it be writ - ten.   So let it be done.

I'm sent here by__ the cho - sen one.__

So let it be writ - ten.   So let it be done.__

To kill the first__ born phar - aoh son.__   I'm creep - ing death.

*2nd, 3rd & 4th times bass drum & hi-hat rest on beat 1.

Play 4 times

Free time

grad. rit.

Additional Lyrics

2. Now, let my people go, land of Goshen.
   Go, I will be with thee, bush of fire.
   Blood running red and strong down the Nile.
   Plague. Darkness three days long, hail to fire. *(To Chorus)*

3. I rule the midnight air, the destroyer.
   Born. I shall soon be there, deadly mass.
   I creep the steps and floor, final darkness.
   Blood. Lamb's blood, painted door, I shall pass. *(To Chorus)*

THE CALL OF KTULU

Music by James Hetfield,
Lars Ulrich, Cliff Burton
and Dave Mustaine

Guitar solo

46

Play 3 times

*2nd & 3rd times play ♪♩ on crash & ride on beat 1.